Giorgio Bolla

The Metaphor

From poetic action to philosophical concept

Translated by Carolina Migli Bateson

The shadow of the sun only,
it's what remains

I never thought that a philosophical essay on metaphor could be analized in a cafe' in Venice.

In fact, the pace of the Lagoon fits perfectly to the internal rhythm of this unconventional work.

This book moves in waves of thoughts.
Just like the waves, it starts off by a small motus, it grows and flows into the peak wave that digs the bottom of the lagoon; then as a gift, it pours it back.

If at that time you are lucky enough to be on the water, you budge.

This essay is itself a metaphor.

Carolina Migli Bateson

There are at least 15 mobile phones belonging to the author at the bottom of the Venetian Lagoon.

CHAPTER I

Who knows weather St. Francis of Assisi understood that his reality, his religion of things, was nothing but an extraordinary sequence of metaphors.

Going back in thought to the highest metaphor, the divinity one, man is forced to reinvent colours , seasons and the acts that condition our life and make it fruitful.

Metaphor is like an act, like a gesture of will power, it's a research, in the end, for freedom.

Reality reinterpreted.

Altissimu, onnipotente, bon Signore,
tue so' le laude, la gloria e l'honore et onne benedictione .
Ad te solo, Altissimo, se konfano,
et nullo homo ène dignu te mentovare .
Laudato sie, mi' Signore, cum tucte le tue creature,
spetialmente messor lo frate sole,
lo qual'e' iorno, et allumini noi per lui .
Et ellu e' bellu e radiante cum grande splendore:
de te, Altissimo, porta significatione .
Laudato si', mi' Signore, per sora luna e le stelle:
in celu l'ài formate clarite et pretiose et belle .
Laudato si', mi' Signore, per frate vento
et per aere et nubilo et sereno et onne tempo,

per lo quale a le tue creature dài sustentamento .
Laudato si', mi' Signore, per sor'aqua,
la quale e' multo utile et humile et pretiosa et casta .
Laudato si', mi' Signore, per frate focu,
per lo quale ennallumini la nocte:
ed ello e' bello et iocundo et robustoso et forte .
Laudato si', mi' Signore, per sora nostra matre terra,
la quale ne sustenta et governa,
et produce diversi fructi con coloriti flori et herba .
Laudato si', mi' Signore, per quelli ke perdonano
per lo tuo amore
et sostengo infirmitate et tribulatione .
Beati quelli ke 'l sosterrano in pace,
ka da te, Altissimo, sirano incoronati .
Laudato si', mi' Signore, per sora nostra morte corporale,
da la quale nullo homo vivente pò skappare:
guai a quelli ke morrano ne le peccata mortali;
beati quelli ke trovarà ne le tue sanctissime voluntati,
ka la morte secunda no 'l farrà male .
Laudate e benedicete mi' Signore et rengratiate
e serviateli cum grande humilitate .

[Francis of Assisi – "The Canticle of all creatures"]

[I]

To whom are these verses , these praises addressed , if not to Him , everyman's God.

The metaphor of selfless help , the result of pure goodness.

*"Most High, all-powerful, good Lord,
all praise is yours, all glory, all honour,
and all blessing ."*

However, it is an unreachable entity, because it is the highest and the most remote. Mortal man, who has been gifted with death, will never come to touch divine purity: even though the metaphor is clear.

*"To you, alone, Most High, do they belong.
No mortal lips are worthy to pronounce your name."*

Is it perhaps the sun that mediates this distance, although it is an intellectual distance that could crush us: the luminous sphere is benevolent and opens our minds to the virtual relationship with the divinity.

A search through light.

*"All praise be yours, my Lord, through all you have made, and first my lord Brother Sun,
who brings the day; and through whom you give us light.
How beautiful is he, how radiant in all his splendour;
of you, Most High, he bears the likeness."*

In Psalm 146 God counts the stars and he can call them one by one: the sky is where the sacred conversation takes place.

*"All praise be yours, my Lord, through Sister Moon
and the stars; In the heavens you have made them,
bright, and precious, and fair."*

The relationship between man and the rest of creation that surrounds him inevitably comes out.

This is the moment for Beauty, always dispensed by God, where man can finally take part in person.

*"All praise be yours, my Lord,
through Brothers wind and air, and fair and stormy,
all the weather's moods, by which you cherish all that you have made.
All praise be yours, my Lord, through Sister Water,
so useful, humble, precious and pure."*

Water becomes the sublimation of created things; the hypothetical escape from the mundane world.

*"All praise be yours, my Lord, through Brother Fire,
through whom You brighten up the night.
How beautiful is he, how cheerful !Full of power and strength."*

The man of God is necessarily strong, because his research of the present, the "here and now" is challenging but imbued with great honesty. He searches through things, fearful at the beginning he becomes fearless while looking for the physical, organic, earthly contact with them.

*"All praise be yours, my Lord, through our Sister
Mother Earth, who sustains us and govern us,*

and produces various fruits and with coloured flowers and herbs."

Itistheman'ssearch:asearchforhisfellowman,asearchforGod.

Could it be the right search in order to exorcize death?

Giving life to death is the sacred metaphor used, desired and imagined the most.

The need for Good is the key, the winning choice.

"All praise be yours, my Lord, through those who grant pardon for love of you;
through those who endure sickness and trial.
Happy are those who endure in peace,
by You, Most High, they will be crowned.
All praise be yours, my Lord, through Sister Death,
from whose embrace no mortal can escape.
Woe to those who die in mortal sin !
Happy those she finds doing your will !
The second death can do them no harm.
Praise and bless my Lord, and give him thanks
and serve him with great humility."

The search for Beauty is the search for Truth; the day of the Lord is the end of a journey of beauty.

Everything is metaphor.

And if the mind runs fast, slow the soul is.

[II]

CHAPTER II

If the metaphor is the desire to follow or to travel the wide streets of thought - if that is true - clearly it is with Philosophy that this search -a search for a definite explanation, hidden to mankind's freedom- is born.

Ion, bard poet possessed by God it is an example /In the following extract Ionis, bard poet is possessed by God.

As Art and Poetry, the Metaphor is as an inexplicable gift from above, from what is elusive and certainly inexplicable. It is as a superhuman dispersion, transcendent, divine indeed.

SOCRATES : "... *You have literally as many forms as Proteus; and now you go all manner of ways, twisting and turning, and, like Proteus, become all manner of people at once, and at last slip away from me in the disguise of a general, in order that you may escape exhibiting you Homeric lore .And if you have art, then, as I was saying, in falsifying your promise that you would exhibit Homer, you are not dealing fairly with me .But if, as I believe, you have no art, but speak all these beautiful words about Homer unconsciously under his inspiring influence, then I acquit you of dishonesty, and shall only say that you are inspired .Which do you prefer to be thought, dishonest or inspired ?"*
ION : *"There is a great difference, Socrates, between the two alternatives; and inspiration is by far the nobler !"*
SOCRATES : *"Then, Ion, I shall assume the nobler alternative;*

and attribute to you in your praises of Homer inspiration, and not art ."
[Plato – "Ion",541E-542B]

We must try to rearrange, bring back the divine or metaphorical thought that lies within the flow of logical science, of human interpretation.

"It is a great matter to observe propriety in these several modes of expression, as also in compound words, strange (or rare) words, and so forth but the greatest thing by far is to have a command of metaphor .This alone cannot be imparted by another; it is the mark of genius, for to make good metaphors implies an eye for resemblances ."
[Aristotle – "Poetics" ,59a]

[III]

Is it a continuous indefinite pursuit of a philosophical sense or a reinterpretation of nil?

Is it the word of Dionysus or the deception of science?

"The world is always as the achieved liberation of God, the vision eternally changing, eternally new of the being more suffering, more opposed, more full of contradictions who knows how to free oneself solely by means of the illusion: even if arbitrary, idle, imaginary these rich metaphysics peculiar to artists .The essential thing into them is the decisive revelation of a courageous spirit who, one day, will take up a position against the interpretation and the moral meaning of existence ."
[F . Nietzsche – "Thus spoke Zarathustra" ,part IV°]

A story beyond the limits of time, an unavoidable need for meaning.

"For the real poet the metaphor is not a figure of speech,rather it is a substitutive image that offers to him concretely,instead of an idea ."

For the philosophers Larkoff[1] and Johnson[2], metaphor means not only the fundamental mechanism for what regards everyday language, but here much more: the cortex, the fundamental basis of the very process of knowledge.

"For the real poet the metaphor is not a figure of speech,rather it is a substitutive image that offers to him concretely,instead of an idea ."
[F . Nietzsche – "The birth of tragedy" ,Ch. 8]

In order to speak, and thus to think, we must make a mandatory choice to adopt metaphorical mechanisms and modalities: the metaphor is the linguistic tool that better than any other expresses our bodily interaction with the outside world. Therefore, thought and language are defined and conditioned by our perceptual structure; to encounter a thought and language disembodied and free of metaphoric gestures is impossible, even in everyday life.

In Paul Ricoeur[3]'s philosophy the symbol lives in the core of hermeneutical reflection, symbol-dream like "the region of the double sense." Interpretation is the mental modus, the key to move from the obvious meaning to one which is latent, hidden from immediate perception. In the metaphor the figurative sense of the human experience is expressed; for example, this happens in the literary language. Through metaphor, a place of creation and truth', we will experience the metamorphosis of language and the metamorphosis of reality'. The "spark of meaning" is the living metaphor; metaphorical statement "as a poem in miniature".

In Jacobson[4]'s philosophy "the principle of similarity is the basis of poetry. . . , prose, however, proceeds essentially by relations of contiguity. Thus metaphor for poetry and metonymy for prose constitute the point of least resistance, and this explains how the research on poetic tropes are oriented primarily toward metaphor. "Truth of metaphor , re-description of reality and even of our being-in-the-world.

"The original form of experience, "the natural image of the world" is this the metaphor? Or is it just a Rilkean "sinking" ? This is Cassirer's thought, but Wittgenstein instead thinks that we always give ourselves an image: not the logical one, not a represent able one; but still we give ourselves a representation.

Cassirer[5], again, argues that the image of the world is richer then language, then myth, then knowledge. It is the ray of light is not yet refracted on the various means of sense; it can be called an intuitive experience, not reflexive. As Kant speaks of the ideal of space and time, and these identities are the intuitive access, so the turn of idea presupposes the turn to the symbolic form, to the meaning.

The struggle of language, of myth ,of Art, of knowledge, of religion manifests itself throughout the will to forge the world ; in religion there are stages where the demoniac, the hallucinatory, fantastic moment blooms.

Everything as the aim without a purpose.

What counts, then ,is "becoming the form": this is the shape of the world's natural image. For the poet it is the entrance to the "sinking" to interior space, place for memory . In this case also Heidegger quotes Rilke.

There are no limits placed upon the intuitive moment, thus it becomes infinite. But all metaphysic has its roots in experience, as its interpretation. Language is , thus, the instrument of this interpretative process, language becomes the foundation of symbolic forms.
Ultimately we speak of "symbolic consciousness", where the symbol is the meaning. Through the signifier is given, is built, the being itself; it also poses a fundamental symbolic

nature of knowledge itself.

Metaphor of words and metaphor of space and time.

The symbol produces forms and thus reality.

Wittgenstein[6] suggests to disguise the thought with language, Cassirer claims that language is both myth and knowledge. The shape of symbol produces itself, the meaning and the original phenomenon of the symbolic function constitute the history of consciousness and metaphysics of the world's reality.

[IV]

CHAPTER III

[V]

METAPHORS OF NIL

You had been at me
I led you
to see the river .
Where is the water
of your run ;

we go together again,
rosy domes
tonight
beyond our
images
sweet by azure sugar,
like the angelical
wings .
Every time at the end of the day,
and then I don't know if the night is
more fine than dawn,
its verity is a land
without paths .
Bizarre angel,
you march over the roofs of dreams,
I picture to myself your
run was wearing the time
of wish .

***

The shadows of the wind
rumble the plains
in campaniles made
by shining ochre .
To dazzle the stones
of the sun
is an easy work
for a poet,
to dig the play
of memories

works the sense
of lost falsehoods .

***

It's happened,
during the other night .
The valley-dweller wind
called for
the mountain wind,
a fast jump
of the voice
in the weak silence
of night .
The life gets away
the load
of appearance .

***

The day is thirsty
when the migrant birds are
seeking for
salty airs
by then finished a few days ago .
To favour the way,
or the flight,
as is the quiet practice among
they who bring the carriage
of their own lives .
I can't see you
and that is like leaving

the colours of return,
wet with the water
of the questions .

***

The wing was staying
in the sun
while the defenceless air goes in
the gilt contrast
of the faces .
The flower has carried
under the wings
and now they chase the mind,
when the soul is still alive
in the air .

***

The night is coming
and the Moon with its own
white border
talks about its
old nights
past between disdain
and beauty,
chasing the road
made by the sky
upon the words
of men .

*

[VI]

CHAPTER IV

As part of reality which connections are made by quantum theory, the laws of nature do not lead to a complete determination of what happens in space and time; the occurrence (within the frequency bands determined by means of connections) is rather put back in the game of chance "

[W. Heisenberg - "Über quantenmechanische Kinematik und Mechanik," Mathematische Annalen, 1926].

The liveliness of chaos, of disorder, the triumph of entropy? Goethe was right, then, in saying that the beauty of the universe lies in its chaos?

Nothing is certain, everything is indeterminate, or, at most, probable. Heisenberg's Uncertainty Principle splits beliefs: where is the metaphor, of which reality is it actually the ghost of?

The principle proves the impossibility of determining the state of position and the momentum of an elementary particle like the electron, the building block of life and of the real cosmos by means of analysis and observation.

Sudden and violent dichotomy between micro and macrocosm?
Is the world we live in, the air we breathe, false, purely virtual?
Thousands of years of beliefs, where I seek or find my metaphors?

Folly of science, unpredictable Lady of the known world and selfish mistress of knowledge.

Wave/particle duality and non-place: nothing more catalogued with human categories of space and time and Man loses his unique ability to foresee his own life and even that of the universe Metaphor of the metaphor, perhaps.

The formula is: $\Delta x \Delta p \geq \dfrac{h/2\Pi}{2}$

in which Δx is the error on the position and Δp the one on the amount of motus while $h/2\Pi$ is the reduced Planck constant.

After all it is the error that might explain things; but then this parallel reality of metaphor ears more meaning, thus the poets are right!

How foolish we are, convinced that eventually we will come to understand. And instead the non-analysis raises its head, and smiles at the Solons' futile efforts and at the funny samples of securities.

"Life flies, and never stays an hour, and death comes on behind with its dark day, and present things and past things embattle me, and future things as well: and remembrance and expectation grip my heart, now on this side, now on that, so that in truth, if I did not take pity on myself, I would have freed myself already from all thought . . . "
[F. Petrarch– "The Canzoniere", CCLXXII]

[VII]

CHAPTER V

Now, before the ending of the day
I roll up the skin
of my paths
or I chase the colour
of waiting,
towards the corner
of the world .

***

The night was ended,
seek the sound
which the Mattutino
places to the throne
between trunks and lights
below the campaniles
and into the grey
rock
I open the space .

***

Under the vaults
made with incense
I crown the poors
with the victory
and over your mouth

my koss
runs .
Look for the yoke
of heart
close by the meadows,
crossed in the mud
of mountain horses .

***

Song of entry
or aristocracy
of the dream
now these your prayers
break the significance
of things .

***

The ramparts of woods
under the heavens of clouds
I move and I go along
the yoke
of the time
I comply with your
desire of delight
and you ignore
the verity
of the dawn .

***

The derisions of death and life
the soiled ramparts
of sun
approach masks
to look at oneself,
into the sacred place
of the metaphor .

***

[VIII]

CHAPTER VI

With good certainty, one day, we will demonstrate that also animals are able to dream and we will know what their symbolic -or metaphorical- world is.

The brain structures are the result of an evolutionary path in the same way as the rest of the organic world , therefore the oldest areas have found their anatomical and functional contact with the most recent formed areas within evolution.

Does a metaphorical brain exists?

The arcus and the paleocerebello, for example, are involved in the sensation of near-death, they form the basis of so-called symbolic area of the brain, which is integral part of the corpus callosum.

This structure connects the "dominant" left hemisphere that has the function of language processing, with the right, which seems intended for the pursuit of artistic and symbolic mediation of the individual.

A lesion of the corpus callosum - "split-brain" - implies a disconnection and a more obvious freedom of the right hemisphere: the individual is not aware of information that come from that hemisphere, the brain region is "dumb" and the interpretative and perceptive processes do not reach awareness.

It is the frontal cortex, which collects and sorts the "primordial" afferents as departure from the sub-cortical areas of the emotional limbic system that arranges itself in order to surround the corpus callosum.

Neuro-physiological characteristics of these neuronal circuits are to release for a long time, even after the factor that triggers the activity finishes up.

Thus, a recollection/remembrance recently reactivated wakes up in the mechanism of memory and after about half an hour the same sequence of memory images appears in the dream. Perhaps it is the persistence of activation of the circle mnemonic neuronal , with non-removal of the neurotransmitter in the synapse. Posthumous negative image of consciousness.

Therefore there is a metaphor for a parallel and original mental reality, pre -linguistic and symbolic- on language

In this case we can now say that the neuro-physiological study also confirmed that the decision-making unconscious , that is what is not floating in the vast sea of consciousness, sometimes anticipates temporally (for a few seconds) the awareness of our choice - as claimed by John-Dylan Haynes[8] of the Max Planck Institute.

Closer to the dream process then to the "everyday" interpretation one.

[IX]

CHAPTER VII

The world of poetry and the one of the so-called reality are two separate universes: parallel, touching only in the moment of poetic creation, that is the fall into the black hole that makes them communicate. Poetry dries the word and the door to the metaphor.

So it is my poetry in the very moment it is written, it has already become the subject, it is already dead. It lives no longer.

THE MEMORY AND THE ACT

I entered. The heavy door that I had just passed was, I think, one of many XVIIth century (or maybe XVIIIth century) palaces of Bologna that mightily lap all the roads radiating out of the heart of the city. Aristocratic houses, very high, with immense roofs and internal wide steps staircases, short and dusty. Above the head monochrome frescoes almost always of a sacred or mythological type, in laic and middle-class residences.

The entire city background colour, the red brick alternating with ochre yellow: the colours of the earth and the healthy feeling of the people of Emilia. I had not realized the reason why I wanted to get in. In my youthful wanderings through the cities close by I used to find the origin and the satisfaction of an innate spontaneous solitude , without cerebral frills.

Maybe I was already tired of the assemblage of bodies and ideas.

The door was extremely heavy and it was naturally - dramatically- open. I tucked the huge stairs and then I began to see and touch physically (almost eating) the dust that permeated and dominated the environment itself.
Gray powder, which had its own colour persisting even when raised in the still air above time.
I stopped on the first landing and sat down.

This scene in memory , by trying to looking for suitable circuits to bring back that moment, does not allow me to remember how much physical human time, I was so in that hall, feeling carefully the confirmation of the absence of other people who could climb the stairway or come out from one of the doors of the apartments. Huge palace, it had trapped the air of my questions and fears.
He had begun racing few years back, perhaps as a long unspoken need, now expressed. That pilot friend of mine , stuck in the world of construction and fittings, had restored a large building of his own city - Bologna. And made there his own new home.

That evening I arrived at the housewarming with my partner at the time, I spent an normal evening with a few friends met mostly that same evening, standing up, eating those things that you absolutely hate.
Everyone saying: "what a beautiful home, modern and an-

tique at the same time.". it was true, he really did a good job, certainly a very expensive-almost too much- one.

Pleasant evening, useless. Now, after several months, only now, I understand. The sense of it has surfaced to my consciousness.

It was the palace of youth, on a cold lonely day in a beloved city. The sense of it was just that, but on that evening , coming back I did not understand.

[X]

Memory had decided I had to figure it out later, much later: as if the act of climbing a dusty stairway would want to remain hidden until the sudden arrival of a mental light in a dull Sunday afternoon, between one sad thought and the other.

Entering the building is the entrance into something that is not yours and you are, in spite of yourself, forced to understand. It is the metaphor of entrance, the desire for knowledge.
In this way the metaphor is experienced, acted out, remembered, and it remains beyond the same will.
It is a method of mind, a psychological gesture even before the rational one, aimed to explain the reality of things: a reality that "normally" we can never penetrate to the end. It is as the other side of the coin, or the reality that is. It is the result of the first interpretation, beyond the senses and well ahead of rational devastation .

SIGISMUND : "That is true :then let's restrain
This wild rage, this fierce condition
Of the mind, this proud ambition,
Should we ever dream again :
And we'll do so, since 'tis plain,
In this world's uncertain gleam,
That to live is but to dream :
Man dreams what he is, and wakes
Only when upon him breaks
Death's mysterious morning beam .
The king dreams he is a king,

And in this delusive way
Lives and rules with sovereign sway ;
All the cheers that round him ring,
Born of air, on air take wing .
And in ashes (mournful fate !)
Death dissolves his pride and state :
Who would wish a crown to take,
Seeing that he must awake
In the dream beyond death's gate ?
And the rich man dreams of gold,
Gilding cares it scarce conceals,
And the poor man dreams he feels
Want and misery and cold .
Dreams he too who rank would hold,
Dreams who bears toil's rough-ribbed hands,
Dreams who wrong for wrong demands,
And in fine, throughout the earth,
All men dream, whate'er their birth,
And yet no one understands .
'Tis a dream that I in sadness
Here am bound, the scorn of fate;
'Twas a dream that once a state
I enjoyed of light and gladness .
What is life ?'Tis but a madness .
What is life ?A thing that seems,
A mirage that falsely gleams,
Phantom joy, delusive rest,
Since is life a dream at best,
And even dreams themselves are dreams ."

[P. Calderón de la Barca- "Life is a dream",Act II°-Scene XVIII°]

[XI]

Poetry as a metaphor, diving in a maze that is symbol of search - truth, beauty,. . . - Totally celibate, aimless, functionless. Because the poetic image is necessarily the result of a conceptual intervention (perhaps then the noblest), while the visual image is immediate, sensory.

PROSPERO : "You do look, my son, In a mov'd sort, as if you were dismay'd: be cheerful, sir .Our revels now are ended .These our actors, as I foretold you, were all spirits, and are melted into air, into thin air: and, like the baseless fabric of this vision, the cloud- capp'd towers, the gorgeous palaces ,the solemn temples, the great globe itself, yea, all which it inherit, shall dissolve, and, like this insubstantial pageant faded, leave not a rack behind .We are such stuff as dreams are made on; and our little life is rounded with a sleep .Sir ,I am wex'd; bear with my weakness; my old brain is troubled: be not disturb'd with my infirmity: if you be pleas'd, retire into my cell, and there repose: a turn or two I'll walk, to still my beating mind ."

[W. Shakespeare– "The Tempest",Act IV°-Scene I°]

XII

The dream creates the dream, the awareness of a different reality (more pure and more profound?) annihilates the strong thought of the first explanation of things.

"The purpose which guided him was possible, though supernatural, certainly. He wanted to dream a man: he wanted to dream of him with minute completeness and impose him on reality .That magic project has exhausted the whole space of his soul; if only someone was asking his name or every feature of his previous life, he didn 't succeed in answering .He had better the desert and falling temple,

since it was a little part of visible world; even he had better the nearness of the woodsmen, as they charge oneself with satisfaction of his frugal needs .The rice and the fruit of their tribute were enough for his body, exclusively devoted to sleep and dream . . . .

He realized that the engagement to shaping the incoherent and dizzy substance of which the dreams are made up is most arduous that a man could undertake, even though he would be good at piercing all the riddles of the superior and inferior Order; this deed is much more arduous than the weaving of a sandy rope or the coinage like stamp of the soulless wind .He realized that an initial failure was unavoidable ."

[J. L. Borges – "The circular ruins"]

Conceptual form as picture: Castel del Monte, the hunting castle of Frederick "Stupor Mundi".

The path to liberation, the purity of form or materialized metaphor as an image. Meta-dream* as a memory of the dream.

[XIII]

*Metadream: Giorgio Bolla's neologism "the dream within the dream".

Ange fumbles for
my hands
inside the nights constellated
with the phantasms
of metadream,
shapes of hills
in the snow
of the fury
or the sweetness .

[XIV]

Giorgio Bolla is a surgeon, pilot and poet.
He published six books and earned numerous awards

2011 Grand Prix of Poetry Mediterranean [Larissa - Greece].
2012 Special Act Award for the Veneto "AMBIART" to the poem "Salite."

2013 Second Prize in the "International Poetry Competition 2012-2013 - Seeking for a poem" [Sarajevo] with the poem "Climbs".

His poetry has a life of itself. It pours out in complete freedom and adopts the poet, as its vessel, its instrument .

Giorgio is 'a constant seeker of beauty.

Carolina Migli Bateson is an actress, a theatre director and a translator. Graduated in 1995 at the Gaiety school of Acting, Dublin, she works and lives between Italy Ireland and U.K. She hates talking in third person.

ICONOGRAPHY

I)   To exorcize death

II)   The light breaking through the world

III)   Penetrating a parallel dimension

IV)   Human solitude

V)   The endless pursuit

VI)   The subjectiveness of space-time

VII)   The journey

VIII)   Vague velocity

IX)   The melody into emptiness

X)   Will You have any more?

XI)   Like life, like death

XII)   Beauty and purity

XIII)   The pureness of shape

XIV)   The foolish question

Pictures

I, IV, V, VI, VII, VIII, IX, X, XI, XII, XIV by Fabio Sercia

II, III   by Giorgio Bolla

XIII   by Alfredfo De Giovanni

Notes

Translations

- Francis of Assisi translated by Anonymous

- F. Petrarch trans. by A.S. Kline

- P. Calderón de la Barca trans. by D.F. MacCarthy

- Plato trans. by B. Jowett

- Aristotle trans. by S.H. Butcher

- F. Nietzsche trans. by the Author

- J.L. Borges trans. by the Author

Figures

[1] **George P. Lakoff** is an American cognitive linguist, best known for his thesis that lives of individuals are significantly influenced by the central *metaphors* they use to explain complex phenomena.The metaphor thesis, introduced in his 1980 book *Metaphors We Live By* has found applications in a number of academic disciplines and its application to politics, literature, philosophy and mathematics .

[2] **Mark L. Johnson** is Knight Professor of Liberal Arts and Sciences in the Department of Philosophy at the University of Oregon. He is well known for contributions to embodied philosophy, cognitive science and cognitive linguistics, some of which he has coauthored with George Lakoff such as *Metaphors We Live By*. However, he has also written extensively on philosophical topics such as John Dewey, Immanuel Kant and ethics.

[3] **Paul Ricœur** was a French philosopher best known for combining phenomenological description with hermeneutics. As such his thought is situated within the same tradition as other major hermeneutic phenomenologists, Martin Heidegger and Hans-Georg Gadamer.

[4] **Daniel Jacobson** works on a range of topics in ethics and moral psychology, especially issues concerning sentimentalism and the moral and political philosophy of J.S. Mill, and he has published extensively in these fields as well as

in aesthetics and political philosophy. Jacobson is currently working on the Mill volume for the Routledge Philosophers Series and a collaborative book project, *Rational Sentimentalism*, with Professor Justin D'Arms (Ohio State) for Oxford University Press.

[5] **Ernst Cassirer** was a German philosopher. Trained within the Neo-Kantian Marburg School, he initially followed his mentor Hermann Cohen in attempting to supply an idealistic philosophy of science; after Cohen's death, he developed a theory of symbolism, and used it to expand phenomenology of knowledge into a more general philosophy of culture. He is one of the leading 20th century advocates of philosophical idealism.

[6] **Ludwig Josef Johann Wittgenstein** was an Austrian-British philosopher who worked primarily in logic, the philosophy of mathematics, the philosophy of mind, and the philosophy of language. Wittgenstein's influence has been felt in nearly every field of the humanities and social sciences, yet there are widely diverging interpretations of his thought.

[7] **Max Karl Ernst Ludwig Planck**, was a German theoretical physicist who originated quantum theory, which won him the Nobel Prize in Physics in 1918. Planck made many contributions to *theoretical physics*, but his fame rests primarily on his role as originator of the quantum theory.

[8] **John-Dylan Haynes** has studied psychology and philosophy from 1992 to 1997 at the University of Bremen. Since 2006 he teaches neuroimaging at the Bernstein Center for Computational Neuroscience Berlin.

He also heads a research group at the Max Planck Institute for Cognitive and Brain Research in Leipzig.

His studies mainly concern the neural basis of consciousness in the visual and motor processes.

Sommario

CHAPTER I	9
CHAPTER II	16
CHAPTER III	22
CHAPTER IV	27
CHAPTER V	30
CHAPTER VI	33
CHAPTER VII	36
Figures	52

@ Giorgio Bolla Gennaio 2016
@ Mnamon Gennaio 2016
ISBN 9788869490170